Jackie —
you know
thank you for

Nov 6/01

THERE WILL BE BLOOD
& I WILL TELL YOU
PUT YOUR HAND
DOWN HERE

By

BETH EVEREST

National Library of Canada Cataloguing in Publication

Everest, Beth
        There will be blood & I will tell you put your hand
down here / Beth Everest.

(Palm poets series)
ISBN 0-88753-388-4

        I. Title. II. Series.

PS8559.V46T44 2004   C811'.54   C2004-901861-2

The Palm Poets Series is published by Black Moss Press at
2450 Byng Road, Windsor, Ontario N8W 3E8. Black Moss
books are distributed in Canada and the U.S. by Firefly Books,
3680 Victoria Park Ave., Willowdale, Ont. Canada. All orders
should be directed there.

Black Moss would like to acknowledge the generous support
of the Canada Council and the Ontario Arts Council for its
publishing program.

Le Conseil des Arts | The Canada Council
du Canada | for the Arts

ONTARIO ARTS COUNCIL
CONSEIL DES ARTS DE L'ONTARIO

To Chris, Emily, and Madeleine.

in the garden

you tell me, *you look*
good enough to lick, and i answer
yes, my hands tied to the cinnamon
tree.

your tongue splits me and i watch my
belly grow. you release my wrists, the lashes
stained open. all of me is flowing into
deltas. my belly swells into a globe, black earth
wet with sweat of deep green grass. you are lost
in this landscape, my own earth. your mouth, astonished,
cannot utter a word

for you, i squeeze my belly to the size of a pea,
hold it to the light so that we can see its
lakes and mountains. we are its drop of water
the erotic blue on the lip
of a crevasse. look.

5

never before have i loved

like this: his hands at my
throat, sharp nails
smell of the earth
his hands tighten and tighten,
smell the earth as they tighten,
and as my breath begins to stop,
it stops, it bottles inside, fills
my lungs, i fill up. i expand, i
expand, i feel like, i feel, i, as
the blood expands, begins to
drip to flow, to flow to run, i
ooze out the top of his
squeezing hands.

6

christmas in England

i find no warmth so i run a hot bath. 6 cm
of water. a room full of steam. i cannot see
the window which overlooks the garden,
the chestnut trees, the dying elm. but
i know the view will be limited
by the rain

i can see nothing, but my hands seem to rise
out of the thick air, then balance suspended,
wait for me until i am ready. they grasp
the cold edge of the tub, lift me while i
shift my body. in. the water scalds my feet
and i try to blanket myself with its heat. i lie
down, push my back, my shoulders down and
under, against the grip of the tub

water covers my neck. i look along the length
of me disappearing into the steam. nipples
soft and tender. and cold. breasts
rise above red rings of flesh.

i must tell you

now? i must tell you. is it time?
here, touch my hand. (we
are in this together). lips
part with breath
on your fingers. the child
is (with) me. i am
with my child. you
have given me your hand.
i will hand to you
what is already
mine.

8

print our growing

now, you, here with me, you
who touch the inside with red
hands. reach up. print our growing
on the sides of the walls. we are the pattern
or perhaps pattern prints us and another
pained hand reaches out to touch
another wall, another human, the same
thing (it is the same thing) reaches out to tell
another story, to put a voice to story, to what is
said inside, a voice to what happens. to what
is thought to happen. feel the skin as it sleeps
open, wide as a radiant sun. feel it warm
as a river flow. blue on this cave wall. it is light.
my daughter, watch the mark of our fingers stretch
with each lung breath, heart pound, wing beat. you
are a bird beak. speak in your language. you, my daughter,
are the water, lapping. listen. you are in here with me.
feel my mouth with your blue lips.

the bruise

i am mother. umbilical, find the centre. the bruise is right here. somewhere in the middle. can you feel it? about the size of a fist. i am recounting. counting on you (you, falling from your bicycle, break your arm and i wash your hair, brush curls that cling to your tiny neck like a wet kiss) to keep breathing

later, you fall on the ice, the 2nd break, your ankle. dad, not knowing, not seeing you (my mother) slip as you step from the car, drives away. you sit on the edge of the alleyway, propped against the familiar concrete of the back of the store. dad is inside, serving customers, and you, you cannot go in or out but sit near the back door that you can not reach. women from the church come to clean your house. too much. intrusion. too much for you. you with 6 children, marked by the birth of each. and he said she's so ugly, the birth marking him. what's her name? i am dreaming now. it all blends. my strawberry mark, a unicorn's protruding horn. i prod my daughter's in. come in. my milky breasts ache. i am counting.

counting. the 3rd break. my broken arm. it is a skiing
accident. i put my hands out. i cannot see the wall of
snow, but feel it in front of my face. (i am the daughter
trying to wash her hair, wash her hands, bathe with one
arm outside of the tub). even at 16 i am aware of other
things: that i must be beautiful in order to compete, and if
not beautiful then quick-witted, and if not, then what? i
use the sling that holds up my cast as a secret place. what
can i hide that is less than the length of my arm?
i look in the cupboard. why are we hiding?

you go into your room and lock the door. we have made
you a cake. something. turned it out of the pan
too early, and the pink sponge cracks, crumbles when we
ice it too warm. and now it is cold. i make a cake for your
3rd birthday. there is not enough time. it all blends
(mother, me, daughter). i don't know who
to surprise.

11

blood

blood. i must tell somebody. labour. my story.
is anybody listening? silent hand on the wall
smooth as stone. the red hand. the beginning.
reaching out to touch. this cliff,
smooth stone that i cannot climb. fingertips
read each geological layer: paleozoic. touching
mesozoic. oozing pleistocene. sluicing down and
down. it flows. my feet are in
water. words come in waves. the swelling
of the tide. print the pattern
genesis. i must tell. you, my story.
i am caught in the liquid. 1st.
breath.

12

the dream of birth

i squat in the bare earth
beside the river. globe
of my belly breathes down
between my knees.

i breathe my daughter down
and down until i feel her swim
in the middle distance
between her and me, swimming
but she catches like a salmon hook.
plants herself like an octopus
sprouting limbs. then, with no
more room to contain her growing

she splits me. my uterus
tears down the side. the seam
parts and she pushes her arm
through, elbow 1st, resting it
on the edge as if to test the water

redder with each contraction
she slides her hand through
the opening. trails it in
the liquid of her birth. she wants
to touch the outside
through the inside. her
hand is on the wall, presses
on the inside of my belly, somewhere
in the liminal space. and now
her head appears. eyes look through
my stretched skin

14

but i do not see her
me intent on the river of
her birth.

do i begin

where do i begin a monumental life?
at the imaginary (liquid
be specific. frame it. re-tell.
begin with memory)
or pinpoint, me
eve/il, in my own
narrative, store
of detail: this happens, then
this. logic tells me yes, record it exactly.
it happens. capture con-
sequence. and frame it. be specific.
re-count. re-cord. re-
freeze the event in its fluid

memory mixes with de/
siring of all things known and unknown,
before and after, perhaps long ago.
(liquid. be specific) or maybe not. maybe now.
me now. i am a mother. yes. with (my) child.

15

into that quiet

into that quiet place
where silence bursts with winter light. and now
now. even now
after the tearing of flesh, blood in the snow
cracking of bones. you
you who opened me like a knife
bring me here to this

gentle as an apple blossom
your eyes flutter like summer petals
lips bud into 1st
vowels opening shadows of
that quiet place
that dark of night. i feel
my lungs open, symphonic
operatic.
                    no words
sound into that quiet place
where breathing whispers into warm breath

16

of your / my birth
my tiny daughter, your hands
fisting my breast, for that 1st
word, that silent touch, that
quiet place.

at the top of opal mountain

when i stand on the top
sky blue rippling
cloud, i am at the bottom of the ocean
amongst (mollusks/crustaceans/
echinodermata?), i cannot find the word, though i hold
the fossil in my hand. i know that we are this: this
is us. we are swimming on top of a mountain
(i don't even need to close my eyes) i swim in
to memory, it is liquid. absolute

silence. at 1st i think of blackbirds during
a slow pavan or elegant mating dance but there
is no sound. or dark and brooding
fish of nether waters. but there is no flash
of scales. no ripples of skin. silent long black robes
of monks and they are at least what they appear: i cannot
see their faces, but hear their Trappist silence. watch
from the pew, them each in turn genuflecting, rising,

smoothing across the floor-like stage, soothe
like lines intersecting across this page, they cross
themselves, they form a circle around the
altar of stone. silence. nothing happens
and there is silence. and again nothing. i am in
a Beckett play, and i hold this fossil in my hand

and then from nowhere, from somewhere nearby
a slow note rises and another sings out concentric
rings toward the cathedral ceiling, the clouds
above these mountain peaks, and i feel something
in my throat, my mouth, my lips shaped to form
the perfect, the 1st opening, the very 1st breath.

19

knitting

when i am 6, i learn to knit, and because
we have not yet learned metric, i knit
a turquoise belt 76 inches long, and give
this belt to a 6 yr old who has a birthday
and so she is 7. the 1st of us to change. she
is so thin that it goes around and around
and around her waist, her chest, her arms, her
neck

20

and i knit a sweater for my 1st boyfriend and say
here is something by which to remember. maybe
it hangs in his closet or his mother gives it to the
church for the hungry and needy, or he
unravels it the way we try to
understand our lives,
forgetting and re-membering, twisting
it into a skein of wool
held in 1 hand.

if these are our stories

hand in hand to the library, all 6 of us kids
walking. all 6 sleeping crossways in 1
bed. 6 roped together for the steep
climb to Cavell Meadows. and we climb and
climb and then it is winter so we are pulled
by lengths of rope, our hands burning, our feet
on skis bumping behind the skidoo over the icefloes
and up. and i remember letting go of the line of
hands.

my 1st day of school, and there the lady's red-lipped
smile. and moving to the big house with the
fear of fire. losing my glasses and hand in
hand with the teacher finding them in the
locker room at the swimming pool. and running
with a stick i chase a black bear until he runs away
down the back alley. or is it a shovel?

did i chase the bear with a shovel? or was my
sister the hero, the chaser, and i the chasee?
i remember popsicles saved and melting
in a drawer. i believe that she convinced me
to commit the act, so perhaps she starred in this role too.
perhaps these were her stories, or someone
else's, stored, saved, savored. or was this
even the beginning, someone's beginning
or mine, each remnant being pulled along the line,
each bit coming after and after and
after. the ever after. they lived happily ever
after. or we did.

22

at 10

riding my bicycle down main
street Jasper. i am whistling. i
remember distinctly the position
of my mouth when it hits the pavement
after my elbows skid across the gravel after
i fly over the handlebars after i hit a
pothole after putting my hands in my
pockets. a woman gently lifts up my chin from the
road - and props me up on the curb. gone is
the flesh from under my chin. and the knobs
of my elbows. the front of my t-shirt.
and something
else.

23

no trauma

i lose my 1st tooth when i am 5. big deal.
but i get glasses when i turn 6. and
leave them at the swimming pool when
i am 6 1/2. my grade 1 teacher holds
my hand and we tread back for them.
i remember her calm
mouth moving, *don't worry, dear.*
but my toothless frenzy
continues (by this time i regularly
lose and grow new teeth and it is still
long before the dreams). but it is
the 1st time for my glasses. they
are exactly where i left them. in the
cubicle carefully chosen away from
other girls who might look under
and see me naked. or worse, look
over and see me standing on the
bench avoiding their eyes. no one
looks. please note:
there is no
trauma.

the house

when i am 7, we move to a massive house: unlit
corners and animals that crawl from
walls in the night. the bigger danger, though
is fire

we prepare for the possible—
an emergency, the whole of it
terrifyingly staged. stand at the bottom
of the stairs. each of us takes turns
shouting FIRE. FIRE. our small voices
suddenly awake to this terror. thirsty
flames. crawling along smoke blackened
floor. FIRE we shout. through haze of heat, dark
of not knowing anything at all. each
responsible for single-
handedly waking others with one
desperate cry. and then it is
my turn

i shout and shout and shout until
words burn in my throat.

she wants to see the circus

pins and needles prickle
down one arm and through my left
hip. this time, i find it difficult
to walk to the kitchen, make a cup of tea

i see her face through the window.
her hands press against the glass,
desperate to touch for one last time
her mother. me, who has
abandoned her to this
stranger's car.

she wants to see the circus
and i am too busy doing
something already i have
forgotten. i have packed her
a snack and peanuts to feed the monkeys.
done her hair in ponytails with
red and blue ribbons. given her
a dollar to spend.

once again, i feel her
pressed up against the underside
of my ribs, a cage for her
little girl's body. and now
i see her face against
the window. she does not
see me looking at her. she
concentrates, blows bubbles
of spit, lets them dribble down
the window. i tell her stop.
she does not hear. i reach out
to wipe away the mess. but
it is on the other
side.

in my mother's clothes

i wear the matching skirt and sweater sets that
my mother has neatly preserved in their
original garment bags. this one, a robin's
egg blue, is lined with pure silk. i imagine
her thighs swishing against the material as
her legs move, crossing themselves at the
knee as she sits

and there she is, walking with her mother. the
street photographer mistakes them for sisters.
perhaps this is what entices her, her mother, to
buy the photo, but she slips the card with his
name into her pocket, she finds it later and blushes.
red. my grandmother has long ago married the
man her father hired to thresh the wheat

and what my mother's husband, my father,
thinks of me in these costumes, me in my mother's
clothes, must erase the 30 yrs., melt 1/2 his life away
as he sees me as her, my mother.

28

but i am much more
awkward in the slim skirts, nylon
stockings, the high heels with the toes
pointed toward him, though slightly
inward. and what he thinks he will not say
because he is not a man
of words.

29

fishing

my mother takes us to Seba Beach
where the water is blue as cousin Bentley's eyes
we row out at dawn, dangle our lines
above the seaweed's mossy glade

we will stay at the cabin and so will they, the 7 of us
and 6 of them. we peel away winter boards from the
windows. sweep mice and spiders from under
the beds. he and i are only 11 years old, but yes
we will be the dirty ones, together dig the hole,
haul up buckets of earth, and Mom and uncle Bob
and the other older kids will
transfer the outhouse, slide it across the mud and

Bob and Aunt Edith will sleep in Oma's room, Mom
on the couch and us kids in the attic on coil spring
beds. butterhorns for breakfast
and we will dip for water at the well down the road,
and walk in pairs with a pail slopping between us

we are pink and blue fish in our new
swimsuits. dive off the pier for pennies
that we spend at the store: mojos,
tar babies, shoestring licorice, sugar sticks and popeye
cigarettes. walk back along the lazy shore.
perhaps today we'll climb the cliffs on the back road,
fight a war with sand grenades. get too much sun,
again, and peel sunburned skin off each other's backs
in a single sheet.

31

Bentley rows me out in the boat, the cabin winking like
a spot along the shore. *come and sit with me,* he says, and
i stand, arms out for balance. he takes my hand, feel the
heat of his. don't feel the cut on my foot as i step on
new blood pooling like a sunset
between my feet

Bentley pumps the oars, and the boat bumps through
the water. he delivers me, back
to my mother. i am lying on the kitchen table
mom uses needle and thread, sews the gaping wound
my foot pulsing *come and sit with me*
me still feeling the taste of the heat.

i am 13

i am 13, staying with a friend
in the basement of her house
while parents are away. we
hear a voice at the window. it is
a boy from school, and we, in our thin
cotton pajamas, flirt with him as he
squats down and peers in. it is a summer
of possibility and he looks tanned and
muscular in the august sun

suddenly blood quickens. i see only
his legs, but know from the huskiness
of his voice, there is a man there too. he jokes
with the boy, so my friend says hello,
and i know the smile she saves for times
such as these. *bet you've got a good cunt*
he says and she slams the window, but we
can still hear him through the glass
rape 'em both. if you don't, i will and
he laughs

get the phone she says, her eyes blackened
with her words. and i hold on to
the receiver, my fingers too sweaty
to dial.

34

hunting

i have on most of my clothes.
my 1st real boyfriend doesn't
when my father arrives at the door
carrying a shotgun. he is just back
from hunting up north, needed
a place to stay, thought that he
would surprise me.
and he did.

35

at 18

i am living away from home for the 1st
time. and i do not expect her, my mother, but
the house belongs to her and my father
—they bought it for us—so i should not
be surprised, but i am; they have provided for each
of us. 6 kids. they have been fair

i do not expect her. or maybe i know she is
to visit but i choose not to know. i am cooking
dinner for you. spaghetti sauce bubbles on the stove.
Supertramp: we sing lyrics from the
concert. drink red wine from scrubbed out
pickle jars. my mother arrives. there is pasta
only for 2. she does not know the music.
we do not want her to know.

my sister who knows

my sister who knows
everything walks me hand in hand to school.
Jasper Elementary. she tugs me through the big
orange doors, my outdoor boots skidding down
the hallway and into Mrs. Peter's grade 1
class. room 3. the yellow door. and she, my
sister who knows everything, leaves me
there. i stand and stand. then work my shy
body along the blackboard at the front of the
room. and i wait beside Mrs. Peter's desk

another girl lines up beside me, and we stand
there with our backs to the blackboard but
looking only down at the grey/ white tiled floor.
our feet, too big, do not move. we stand.
in new clothes, all of us, it is the 1st
day of school, my purple dress, the white
daisy buttons. the crotch of my tights
already pulls closer to my knees. and i am
aware that other children line up, follow my
lead, forming the line

a woman enters, comes through the yellow
door. she is the teacher, Mrs. Peters, she
is so much older as she looks at the row of
6 yr olds. smiles, curls up her lips stained
red, she laughs and gestures toward the neat
rows of desks and those few children already
seated, those who already know. and she laughs
and she laughs
her lips stained red.

38

4 months pregnant with her

i am sleeping, but my alarm wakes me. i
try to brush my teeth but all my teeth are
loose. the brush wiggles them back and forth.
they begin to come out, 1 at a time. this
is not a product of pregnancy; i have
dreamed variations before

the 1st tooth is perfect and round and smooth
and each succeeding one i savor in my mouth,
the oyster of perfect pearls. and i place the
tooth in a dish at the side of the sink, and
the dish fills with more and more of my perfect
teeth. and as the dish fills, the taste becomes
less and less perfect as more and more teeth
fall. taste becomes more and more like
grit. and now the teeth come quick. more
quickly, my mouth exploding in a hot sea of
sand

exhausted, i crawl from bed, go downstairs to
eat my morning cereal. then dress for work. i
put toothpaste on my brush. begin
brushing. rinse, spit out the foam, saliva,
trigger the gag reflex. vomit my breakfast.
again, my morning pattern

i am in my second trimester. supposedly. i do
not feel pregnant
with possibility.

40

variations on the recurring dream

me in a highschool hallway standing naked
before a locker. i can't remember
the combination and class about to
begin. voices breathe
around the corner.
the bell rings.

am chewing fleshy pink double bubble
so much of it i can hardly
close my mouth.
i expectorate
a huge glob
but there
is so
much more it chokes. i pull and
pull more comes out so much more so
sticky it hugs my teeth. 1st one
then another tooth pulls out, then
another and soon i have no more
in my mouth.

1 tooth is loose. i feel it
with my tongue. wiggle.
then worry it with my finger. spit.
easily falls onto my palm. there
is no blood. no one seems worried but
me: it is a natural occurrence but i
am almost 30: too old and too young to
have falling teeth. now, i worry
another tooth. and soon i stare at my
cupped hands full of teeth. my astonished
mouth puckers.

42

the drive to work

7:00 AM. i drive to work. lightly it snows.
garage doors yawn out of the dark, and i think
i have on too many clothes. i feel bulky, but
this morning i have felt no movement in my
belly. perhaps my baby is asleep. perhaps she
holds her breath. or i do.

i turn right and enter the 14th street traffic.
sky washes red. thin lines of blood. Rocky
View Hospital. orange. a sudden urge. bile in
my throat. i pull over to the curb side, open
the door. rush of lights. screaming horns,
mouths wide open. my mouth wide open. red
fleshy tunnels of throat, lungs, vulva. pink
bulge of stomach, heaving. heaving.

43

too bad for you

it's all with the tongue he says. *it
can't touch the teeth but can't be
too far back either.* sticks out
his tongue bending it like a snake
head. i try to imitate the position,
squirrel my tongue inside my mouth,
but my chewing gum shoots straight
out and into the gravel. *can't whistle and
chew* he says and stalks away. a raven
swoops, cocks his heads at the pebble
colored gum. pecks. CRAW CRAW.
flaps mad wings. back. to wherever.
too bad for you, i say. *too bad.*

now it is your turn

now it is your turn, daughter,
bubblegumming your way
downtown in another city
with your thumb out. you have shown
the sign, and, yes, the stranger
stops his car for you, *yes* he says *hop in*
and you do for several miles where there are few
words, and when he reaches his hand
between your knees, you draw your legs up
to your chest, hide your buds of breasts
lean on the silence of
the set of your mouth
until he pulls over, the door opens
and you can say goodbye
to that one

45

you don't have to do this

i sit among the crocuses, the fur
of their purple heads soft along my thigh

water droplets on the trees that
sun shakes into morning fall
like glass and scatter

i sit here like this. legs spread
into light. snow falls gently.
days pass, months
or maybe time stands. still. my breath is
laboured, and from somewhere deep inside
my mother's voice on the eve of my own
spring:

i wanted to see her but i had anaesthetic so they
said i must rest. i thought they were stalling or
lying, that something had gone wrong, terribly, or
why. why? i want to see her. rest, they said. you're
tired, they said. where is she, i said. you had a

46

hard time, they said. where is she, i said. when it's
time, they said. when it's time, they said. and then
finally, finally, as the sun streamed out from behind
the trees like rays of angels, they brought her to me. she
had a crease across her eyes and forceps marks. all
that dark hair and her pudgy hands. this was my own
baby. my very own. i think i cried

it is easter when my bones
crack like an egg, yolk floods
lichen in the stones. fingers feel
warm cool of the dark, my own eve,
and someone whispers. i think i hear
someone calling. her words to me: *you*
don't have to do this if you don't
want.

47

instinctively like fingers

we have been driving for days, i think,
with wipers slapping at the windscreen.
my parents are in the front seat, silent, as
there is no need for talk. mother
opens the thermos to pour my father
a cup of coffee. i smell it hot and
black. i am in the back seat
lulled to sleep by the sweat of
rain. we are under
water. i see them swimming
by the window, the pacific salmon
a thousand miles from their
salty bed. we arrive with them
at Fin Creek. the mother lies in her
middle distance, between the grey of
sky and grey of river stones. she is still,
now, except for the panting
breaths from her swollen sides, her whole
body breathing. i reach into the water

and she kicks furious, kicking out the seeds
of her own living and dying. i withdraw, and watch
until she is still again, and now i approach more
cautiously, my hand reaches down
to touch her bleeding
belly, stroke her silver
skin, massage it smooth, as silk as chocolate.
we do not talk about her impending death, or the
birthing that nearly kills her. there are spaces
in our silent dialogue. and as i read her, she
bubbles, purrs, her tail fins curl around
my hand, instinctively,
like fingers.

canoeing from the headwaters
of the Maligne

we paddle from the headwaters
of the river, my mother and father
in the cedarstrip canoe ahead of
us, making a direct route
along the rocky shores
of Maligne lake, past Spirit Island
and in a day, we arrive,
my friend and i, in the red canoe,
unpack and begin to set up tents,
shake out sleeping bags.
my father has made a fire in a ring
of stones for my mother who
stands at the hearth, a little bit afraid
of the cold. getting there is not enough
it has started snowing. her hands are red,
and outstretched above his gift. she shivers
he opens his jacket to her, slides it off of his back,

50

and in a moment that i have not seen before
from him, or between them, he
wraps it around her shoulders. whispers
something. and i cannot hear
his words.

51

this close to dying

my mother is in the front of the boat
in her Cowichan Indian sweater, the raw wool
insulating her from the wet of rain and spray

she travels this distance, she
alone with her 6 children
holidays at the ocean, Bates Beach
where salmon leap over the bow
of the fishing boats. in early morning fog,
my 3 sisters and 2 brothers
play in the sand, it is my turn
to work the outboard motor and steer
my mother and i through our own bumpy
ocean

she casts, and i trail my hand
in the water. imagine
it bitten off by the dogfish that yesterday
was ours for the finding, already alive
with the sweet smell of decay.

52

i grasp its tail, swing it round
my head like a lasso. chase after
my sister's shrieks for miles down the hot
sand. never before had we been this close
to dying

and now my mother reels in her catch.
the seagull's orange beak towards us, wide for the cry
that will not come. and my mother reels
it closer. its wings dance on the water's surface.
wings beat on the side of the boat. she reels it
closer. and my mother's deft smack
with the back of her oar. then
with her fingers she plies the hook
from the open throat.

53

my father blindfolds me

my father blindfolds me for something
he and an uncle want to try. as children, we are
perfect pieces for their game. single file at the
top of the stairs, the 1st of us in line taken down
in the dark. it is 1967, air electric with talk about
a man on the moon. our destination. *a journey,*
we are told, *on a ship,* and there is room only for
one passenger at a time. *meet the others there.*
i move to the back of the line, hoping somehow
it will be another year, and i will be somewhere
else, not here, and not waiting for my turn to take
that 1st step and then my sister is led down the stairs.
i am next. i hear it. she screams. *quickly now.*
the scarf over my eyes, led down the stairs, feel carpet's
shaggy threads curling between my toes gripping
like a blinded bird. hear a huge door creak open,
but i must duck down, and i do, *take a step*
up, i am told, so i do, feel a cold rush and i know to stand
very still, crouch down, sit on the backs of my heels.
ship begins to shudder, we are lifting into the centre

of suffocation. i sweat, my whole body sweats,
my toes sweat. i cannot grip on to the hard
plastic floor, cannot hang on even to the familiar.
reach for something to hold, the sides
the walls a door. air pushing
out and i cannot breathe. ship begins to shake, and *Jesus, the
cage is broken,* says someone from a distance, *the whole
is cracked,* voice hollow now, and then right in my ear:
JUMMMP, and before i think, the rush of wind
and my father and uncle are gut screaming laughing,
holding the blindfold and the bench, their ship, that they
have been shaking between them, not seeing me,
me their passenger, in our basement, me.

55

shoes

my husband is talking about shoes, about some
paper he is writing about shoes and i am
thinking about Dad's rubbers, the black
rubber oversoles / overshoes that he always
wears in the rain and the snow. old man's
shoes. things that he must wear. the stamp of
him. the mark that he makes in the snow, in
our lives, in my own life. his father wears them too

56

and i think that i cannot really find the shoe that fits my
mother; perhaps it could be the high heels that are in
the dressup box, the things that are left over from some
other life that we as children never knew, can
never know. but she does not wear these now and
i must imagine her long legs sliding into
white silk stockings. the garter belt that
she throws on her wedding day

all of these scenes i must imagine, as now
most often i remember her in sneakers, but
this is not the right word to describe my
mother's footwear. Ked's? tennis shoes? sensible
flats? glass slippers?

my father wears rubbers, overshoes, like he
has always done because he has always been
old, but my mother i cannot define so simply.
nor can i explain her passion for shoes, stored
in her closet. winter shoes: oxfords, smooth
soled, vibram soled, patent leather, lined in calf
skin, doe skin, sheep skin, nubuck. and her
summer shoes: spiked heels, snakeskin,
western, strappy rainbow, faun, neatly packed
in boxes

i imagine i hear water running for her bath. imagine
the dressing gown folded. her blue cotton nightie,
the large white towel. a new bar of soap. her legs, still
slender, she is upstairs. i know her hand stirs the
water, checks the temperature, she steps
into the bubbles. her feet, narrow,
bumpy. her voice is soft. firm. i hear her call out.
no one answers. i cannot hear her
foot fall on the stair.

58

i haven't held you

i haven't held you like this since you were 4
(she, my mother says this to me), you understand
don't you. it's too difficult to explain. your father.
he doesn't. won't. he's just. you understand don't you.
things are different now, with your generation.
what he's been through. what we have

your father, you understand. no, you understand
nothing. but desire. and how could you? your
father. soil hard and cracked sifting through
sex Wednesdays and Saturdays after church and more
children. there were always more children. we
wanted. i

it's been so long since i've held you. those 10 yrs
of pregnancy. ten wonderful god-awful years, belly
swelling, fish-flopping, children kicking, crying,
years i haven't held you

59

you pull away (still your face - i know you
by your face. you want your father, you always
want. because he gave to you nothing and desire

sober eyes, his dry lips. and the earth
crumbling arthritic through fingers. yes, i suppose
he gave these too. too bad. you've got nothing.
and desire

and now he is old and i am
old. i am nothing too. nothing but an old
old mother holding my baby girl. your
hair is dark while mine grows grey. crumbling.
through fingers.

60

our flesh, our blood

at 5 months pregnant i begin to
bleed. red drops of what
i am afraid is your urgency,
i am afraid
of meeting you too soon.

you turn away from me: the ultrasound
allows me to trace my finger along
your spine, the smooth soles
of your feet and each tiny toe

you turn toward me, your mouth bowed,
your eyes closed, i feel you
move inside of me and i
place the palm of my hand
to the heat.

61

red sky and morning

our 3rd trimester together
has started, and i have painted
every room in the house. i thought
of doing a landscape on the walls
of your room, i imagined bubbling
water over mountain stones, lush mosses, and
dragonflies. i wanted dragonflies and lace,
but i do not have the patience
these days. and i want to have all the projects
finished for your arrival. i have sewn
curtains, made a quilt, and now i am knitting
a sweater for your new body

the problem, though, is size. how do i
estimate the length of your arms, the width of
your shoulders. and i am tired. of sleeping
of waiting, of not feeling your movement
inside of me. of eating. of growing and
looking chubby not glowingly pregnant.

of the sickness and the pain that shoots
up from the base of my spine. of my
skin stretching over what i can only believe
is you

i am a balloon lost in a hurling storm
i am a portal, a hole stretching into red
sky which soon you, my child, will explode
into morning.

63

my shape

my shape is not normal for a
woman 8 month's pregnant. my belly
is not round. it is not a basketball. i do
not feel like a beached beluga. my belly
moves. it is thick jelly. my belly flows. oozes.
juts out at odd angles. it is a tumor with
1000 limbs. it is a gorgon with 100 heads,
its tongues curl and flick. it is a
dragon heaving out air. and it grows. and it
grows. and it grows.

i hold her

i hold my baby in my arms, we are in
the bath and both of us are quite naked. or at least i
remember that she is naked. i assume that
i am also naked because i have no awareness
of the discomfort of sodden clothes. in fact,
i have no awareness of my own
body

i hold her in my arms, but her head is under
water and i lift her out and she rolls over and her
head is under. i call for you but you do not
come. i can hear you downstairs. i call again
and again. i hear you downstairs. her body is
too heavy to hold. i hear you making coffee.
the dishes rattling in the sink. you open the
dishwasher and all the while i am calling,
screaming because i cannot pull this baby out
of the water

i am calling. my throat burns, but you
cannot or do not choose to hear my panic, my
fear, my rage.

have we touched?

i am nothing but a bloated belly, a jellyfish
with 1 gold tooth. i have read all of the
books: this is a baby
inside of me, and that baby and i are in
symbiosis. yeah, right. has
she telephoned? have we spoken? have we
touched?

i am a vessel, a delta to be
excavated. and there will be blood. blood. and i
will say to you, *put your hand down here. no
not there. here.* and i will take your hand,
soak it in the warm thickness, and press it on
the wall. child's paint. to make my mark.
mark me now. your mark. mark my words.
to mark the wall. we are in this together.
hand to me your waiting hand.

66

the wound

the wound on the back of my thigh. swollen,
red, and slit as if from a surgeon's knife. you
are worried and ask if it needs stitching, but
there is no pain. it doesn't bleed.
you ask my mother to look; she draws
nearer. the 2 of you peer close, closer to see
inside. the wound opens and closes like a mouth

she pulls back her shirtsleeves, you help
her, but she reaches inside. i feel her
push aside muscle and flesh. i feel her
inside, feeling in the wound, finding the
source. i feel her grasp on to the bone of my
thigh. and she pulls and she pulls and she pulls.

67

i hear someone call my name

i hear someone call my name and i
awaken that morning in mid-april.
her soft voice calls from the dark.
she speaks again, but i do not
believe that she speaks to me. i wake
again, and through anaesthetized air i see
a bundle thrust toward me. i do not
know/ remember if i take what is
handed to me. i wake again and now
am in the blue room. i am in bed.
the sheets are blue, my gown
is blue, the walls are blue. i am
transformed, utterly.

68

against my sleeping womb

i hold her fevered nakedness in the night, hot
against my sleeping womb. and in the day,
my belly swollen with her aching, her sweating
body clinging to be held, we wrap together
in a blanket, misting in and out of dream. of sleep.
this is how it is. i have changed my clothes
3 times tonight. i hear the clock. tick. 7:45. tick. 7:46
already i have laboured a full day. i am so hot and
so cold that i cannot stop from shaking. nothing is
still, except her movement, now, as she has settled
a little deeper into the recesses of the world that
she knows. doctor orders forceps and announces
the baby is too high. and i feel her shift. she will come
when she is ready. and she moves, i feel her kick
now against the current of her birth. perhaps she
has changed her mind, decided to head back up. and
i ache with the thought of losing her. i feel
a rush of cold air. and something
i mistake for wings.

69

post operative
induction/delirium/induction

strobes of light. images. faces. mostly
ones i have never known or have simply
seen in passing. yet they seem too familiar.
family. Joan? Pat? Clare? my sisters. my
mother? no. no. a man. i cannot see
his face so i visualize it into one that i
want. yet when i try to recall his
expression, the texture, rough smile,
it is less than a phantasm, an over
or underexposure i have saved, stored
with others, equally in/significant
remnants of faces that i see on the bus.
at work. in other crowds of my life.
streams of dis/connected bits swim
like flotsam. interrupt. interject. and
though i push them aside, sweep them
into neat piles, collect them in a story
neatly ordered they float about my head.
bring me down and down. there are stairs.

it is dark. i think i see, and yes, now the shape of a doorway. i go in. or out. a long corridor. stairs. they bring me down and down and down.

landmarks

she starts school, finishes school, has
children of her own. if i see these even in dream
everything somehow returns
to the beginning so i must start again. i am
reading some legal documents and she in a voice
that i have not (yet somehow have) heard
repeats it back to me: *i, Emily / Madeleine*
do hereby. i don't know what else she says.
i try to wake her father to tell him, listen,
it is language, but he too has gone

the way it was...version 1

i am in the hospital surrounded by blue: the
walls, the bed sheets. and i am wrapped in a
blue hospital gown. they, the nurses, bring me
my baby. unbundle her, untie her gown, unwrap
her from her swaddling. they hand her to me.
she arrives naked, red and purple, her arms and
legs, amphibious limbs, curled tight against
the cool air. her feet and hands are purple,
her eyes pinch shut. she makes no sound,
opens her pink round mouth

i too unbundle, untie my hospital gown, let
it fall to my waist, hold her against my
calm white skin. i draw her mouth to my
breast, feel the tickle of her breath, wait
for the initial pulse, our 1st touch skin to
skin, me feeding her feeding
mouth opens and closes. count the rhythms
of her breathing as she drinks in the new
air and my liquid breath.

no, it was this way

a cart rattles down the hall,
through the air thick with night.
light in the opening door. yes, it is
the nurse. she helps me untie my hospital
gown, wet and pasted to my bulging breasts. she
hands me my baby, my baby with eyes and mouth
budding open

they tell me to count and i am not yet awake. i
see someone thrust toward me a package, *your
baby girl* someone says to me because i am the
mother. i reach out to touch her, to hold
her, but she resisting me starts to cry. she
leaves without saying goodbye. she leaves me
on my own. already grown. and i hear my
birthing, her birth crying. but she doesn't
arrive and i have grown and gone. i try to speak
but my mouth opens only
to a 1st sound, something guttural, something
before the beginning of real time, before
real speech.

74

what i am looking to see

in the hospital, 3 days
after her birth. i pull myself from the
bed. my feet slap down on the floor's cold
linoleum, and my legs, still pregnant with
swelling, do not feel like they
belong to me

i lumber down the corridor, awkward in this
new/ old body. past the storage of diapers and
nighties. i think that i should take a few,
fill my bag so that at home my baby will have
something she needs. but my feet don't take
me there. i walk past the shower room, past
the shelves of clinically folded gowns and
towels, but guilty i remain in the filth of
birth. i walk past the nurses' desk. take the
other corridor so that these people do not
see me, but i worry that they will smell
where i have been

i find the nursery. me on my tiptoes, peering
through the window of the door. a nurse reading
a magazine. she looks up. i do not want her
to know what i am looking to see. identical
swaddlings. confusion of bassinets. i do
not know which baby is mine. there is too
much silence. i do not know which baby is
mine.

counting

my fingers: 6 on one hand. i count
again: 7 - no, there are buds of flesh
between each of my 5 fingers. this feels
normal. i am not worried. normal, i know
this. absolutely natural. natural as
counting. natural as ABC

the hands of my newborn daughter. her
fingers curl over mine. the doctor's concentration,
how he holds my baby's left foot in his hand,
smoothes the bottom, allows her toes to spread
and he counts. *webs are common* he says, and he
fades in and out and i ask for more medication

and then he repeats the procedure with the
right foot. smoothes the sole and allows toes
to spread but there are no webs. 5 toes
on each foot. and i am counting. and i count
again.

what?

legs swollen
belly torn

throw her across the bed
rheumy blue eyes question me
what have I done?
what have i
done?

the falling

it is evening when she falls landscaping down stairs
sky scraping like a ferris wheel splash over sparking
leaves over a falling burst quick laugh she is falling
even as spring rain, even, even, it is evening, my
daughter. a gut screaming. how it happens
in the quick of, in the blink of
she falls from the stairs, from a bicycle, from the top
of the roof and opening to the moon
and i feel it all
float down
and down
into my mother's mother splitting open the prairie's
skin, she is bending, dropping down seeds for
harvest, her legs spread against the sun.
and she bears 8 children, 3 girls, not bad, not bad. it is
evening when she falls, bursts like a party
balloon spreading out zodiac against the sky for a
hundred million trillion years and my
mother's mother's mother transplanted Russian gold
glinting Saskatchewan wheat waves

too bad, too bad, another girl
8 already and then the 3 boys.
down and down
floating
past burned white from sun too cold this ice is aging
me and drowning my baby under sky scraping
my baby not breathing my baby
gulping the air to where she
burst quick. sky scraping
like a paper
cut
white
sheet
floats down and down
she is even falling
leaves. i feel her drop
burst quick
a flaming paper white
she is leaving. falling
under me. she is un-
der, uhhhn - der
under, under, under. i feel her

80

burning. i
feel. i feel her
falling.
i feel her
quivering
tongue.

Acknowledgements

An earlier version of "at the top of opal mountain" appeared in *Dandelion Magazine*. An early version of "shoes" appeared in an essay published in both *Journal of Educational Thought* and *Canadian Society for the Study of Education*. "at 10," "no trauma," "variations on the recurring dream" and "too bad for you" began as part of a longer piece called "whistling" which appeared in *The Fiddlehead* and was published in chapbook form by Circle 5 Press.

My thanks are due to Richard Harrison, Marty Gervais, and Misty Elliott.

CONTENTS

in the garden 5

never before have i loved 6

christmas in England 7

i must tell you 8

print our growing 9

the bruise 10

blood 12

the dream of birth 13

do i begin 15

into that quiet 16

at the top of opal mountain ... 18

knitting 20

if these are our stories 21

at 10 23

no trauma 24

the house 25

she wants to see the circus 26

in my mother's clothes 28

fishing 30

i am 13 33

hunting 35

at 18 35

my sister who knows 37

4 months pregnant with her .. 39

variations on the recurring
dream 41

the drive to work 43

too bad for you 44

now it is your turn 45

you don't have to do this 46

instinctively like fingers 48

canoeing from the headwaters
of the Maligne 50

this close to dying 52

my father blindfolds me 54

shoes 56

i haven't held you 59

our flesh, our blood 61

red sky and morning 62

my shape 64

i hold her 65

have we touched? 66

the wound 67

i hear someone call my
name 68

against my sleeping womb 69

post operative induction/
delerium/induction 70

landmarks 72

the way it was… version 1 73

no, it was this way 74

what i am looking to see 75

counting 77

what? 78

the falling 79

Acknowledgements 83